NATIONAL GEOGRAPHIC OUR WORLD

The Four Blind Men

Based on a Folktale from India

by Vikram Gulaty

NATIONAL GEOGRAPHIC LEARNING

CENGAGE Learning·

One morning, four blind men are walking through the jungle. They cannot see the beautiful trees, but they can hear them in the wind. They cannot see the wonderful flowers, but they can smell them.

Suddenly, the men hear a strange
sound. Something is in front of
them. What is it?

The first blind man puts out his hands and touches something. It feels long and strong. It wraps around his arm like a snake.

"It is a snake!" says the man.

The second blind man puts out his hands and touches something. It is thin. It feels like a rope.

"Aha!" says this man. "It is a rope!"

The third blind man puts out his hands and touches something. It feels tall and round.
"This feels like the tree next to my house," says the man. "It is a tree!"

The fourth blind man puts out his hands and touches something. It feels hard and rough.

"This feels like a wall of a house," says the man. "It is a house!"

The blind men start to argue.
"It is a snake!" says the first blind man.
"No, it's a rope!" says the second blind man.

"You are both wrong," says the third blind man.
"It is a tree!"
   "It's a house!" says the fourth blind man.
   "What is it?" ask all the blind men.

Suddenly, the four blind men hear a loud sound.
"Aha!" they all say. "We know that sound. It sounds
like an elephant."

"It *is* an elephant!" the blind men say. "We were all wrong!"

They know now that four people can "see" the same thing in different ways.

Facts About Animal Senses

Some animals have amazing senses.

◄ Butterflies taste with their feet. If flowers and plants taste sweet to a butterfly's feet, the butterfly knows the flowers and plants are good to eat.

Two-thirds of a shark's brain focuses on smell. It can smell the tiniest drop of blood from more than a mile away. ▼

◄ A bat has a special sense of hearing. This helps it hunt. The bat bounces sounds off bugs. Then it hears these sounds. The sounds help the bat find bugs.

The star-nosed mole's sense of touch is five times stronger than people's sense of touch. It uses its funny-looking nose to feel.

Chameleons have a special kind of sight. They can move their eyes in different directions. They can see up and down at the same time! ►

Fun with Senses

Which sense goes with each body part?

hearing   taste   smell   sight   touch

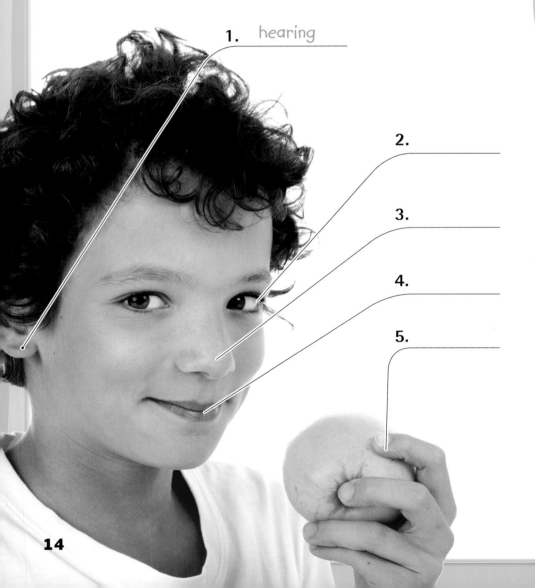

1. hearing

2.

3.

4.

5.

Which word goes with each picture?

hard

rough

loud

beautiful

What else is loud? beautiful? hard? rough?
Use a bilingual dictionary if necessary.

loud _____a crying baby_____

beautiful _____

hard _____

rough _____

Glossary

argue to have a fight with words

blind not able to see

hunt to try to catch something to eat

jungle a place where many plants and trees grow

rope something used to tie things up

thin not wide or fat

wraps covers something around